A WOMAN

"Empowering women to rise, thrive, and lead with fierce determination and grace."

FLEGRA

Table of Contents

1.Introduction to a Woman:

Elegant, resilient, and strong, the female form is one of nature's most magnificent creations. Every facet of life is profoundly impacted by her exceptional combination of strength and tenderness. She fosters connections, advances progress, and shapes society with her unique viewpoints and contributions.

Women have shaped human history and identity in a fundamental way since the beginning of time. Embodying the extraordinary ability to excel in multiple roles at once, they have been nurturers, leaders, artists, pioneers, and warriors. It is impossible to not be inspired and admired by them because of their exceptional multitasking and challenge-adapting abilities.

Women are naturally endowed with an unmatched strength that comes from within. Her resilience is apparent when faced with challenges; she faces them head-on with resolute determination. Her perseverance is evident in the difficulties she faces, as she grows stronger and more competent with every encounter.

The delicate yet profound tenderness that characterizes a woman's nature lies beyond her strength. As she gives loved ones an empathetic, kind, and supportive embrace, her compassion is immeasurable. Each relationship she builds is infused with warmth and love from her, nourishing everyone in her path and fostering a sense of community.

And a world that is more diverse and inclusive is made possible in large part by the viewpoint of women. Her distinct experiences, ideas, and insights provide a fresh perspective on the intricacies of life. She provides an atmosphere where ideas can grow and society can advance by allowing a diversity of voices to be heard.

Women are breaking down barriers and redefining boundaries in every aspect of life, from the home to the workplace. Their steadfast dedication to self-improvement and empowerment sets the path for upcoming generations, encouraging them to pursue greatness and make significant contributions to society.

It is more important than ever to honor and celebrate the achievements of women today. We can build a more equitable and peaceful society by recognizing their achievements, appreciating their difficulties, and pursuing gender parity. Accepting the unique qualities of women opens up countless opportunities for advancement and a better future for everybody.

In conclusion, women are amazing forces in the world because of their many attributes. Her accomplishments inspire, her strength gives her a sense of dignity, and her tenderness and perspective help her shape. A woman's limitless potential should be acknowledged in order to fully embrace and value her influence in all facets of life.

2.Historical Views of Women's Positions;

Women's roles in society have changed and varied significantly over time. Women have occupied a variety of roles and encountered a wide range of expectations and restrictions throughout history and in various cultures. Understanding the historical perspectives of women's positions is critical for understanding the progress made in gender equality as well as the challenges that women still face today.

The position of women varied among ancient societies, including

Mesopotamia, Egypt, and Greece. Some societies restricted women to household roles and denied them political rights, while others permitted them to participate in economic and religious activities. For example, women's rights were restricted in ancient Athens, they were not allowed to own property, and their main responsibility was taking care of the home.

Christianity had a significant impact on how society viewed women's roles during the Middle Ages. The teachings of the Church frequently depicted women as inferior to men, highlighting their responsibilities as spouses, mothers, and housekeepers. This idea strengthened barriers to women's legal rights, employment prospects, and educational opportunities.

A pivotal moment occurred during the Renaissance when novel concepts that contradicted conventional wisdom regarding women's roles surfaced. Renaissance intellectuals like Christine de Pizan promoted women's education by emphasizing their capacity for thought. However, many societies still upheld traditional gender roles, and such ideas were not widely accepted.

Further research on gender equality was conducted during the Enlightenment, when feminist philosophers like Mary Wollstonecraft promoted women's rights. However, major progress toward women's liberation movements and legislative reforms did not come about until the 19th and 20th centuries.

Feminism gained momentum in the 19th century, and activists for women's suffrage demanded equal rights and opportunities. Early in the 20th century, women were granted the right to vote in a number of nations thanks to the suffrage movement's noteworthy victories. Women's roles in the workforce also changed during this time, as more of them pursued financial independence and entered the workforce for pay.

With a focus on topics like equal job opportunities, access to education, and reproductive rights, the women's rights movement continued into the mid-20th century. Significant social and legal changes aimed at advancing gender equality were brought about by feminist activism and consciousness-raising.

Even though women have made significant progress in terms of their legal rights and societal perceptions, obstacles still exist. In numerous domains, including politics, leadership roles, and compensation parity, gender differences persist. Understanding the various struggles that women of various racial, socioeconomic, and physical backgrounds face depends in large part on an understanding of intersectionality.

In conclusion, the status of women in society has changed over time, moving from roles of restriction to a continuous fight for gender equality. Society can move forward with efforts to create a more inclusive and equitable future for everybody by acknowledging the historical perspectives on women's positions.

2.1 Status of Women in Ancient Civilizations;

The social, cultural, and religious beliefs of each society had a significant impact on the status of women, which varied widely throughout ancient civilizations. Certain ancient societies bestowed upon women considerable privileges and prospects, while others restricted their rights and liberties to subservient roles.

Compared to many other ancient civilizations, women had more rights and privileges in ancient Egypt. They could trade, own and inherit property, and even occupy prominent roles in the state and in houses of worship. The roles of

Egyptian women as wives and mothers were highly esteemed, and they were respected for them. Wives and daughters of the pharaohs frequently had powerful positions, and some even rose to become pharaohs themselves.

In contrast, women were mostly restricted to the home in the more patriarchal society of ancient Greece. They were expected to take care of the home and raise the children in accordance with their roles as wives and mothers. Women's rights were restricted, and their access to political and educational opportunities was also restricted. There were, however, a few exceptions where powerful women made a difference, such as in religious cults and via their connections to powerful men.

Compared to Greece, women enjoyed more freedom and social mobility in ancient Rome. They had greater access to educational opportunities, and some of them rose to positions of influence and authority. Roman women were able to manage and own property, conduct business, and take part in social and cultural events. They still had fewer legal rights than men, though, and had to deal with gender norms and cultural expectations of modesty.

Depending on their social and economic origins, women's status in ancient India varied. The Rigveda and other ancient Hindu texts recognized the value and accomplishments of women. On the other hand, women's roles became increasingly determined by their caste and class as social stratification advanced. Lower-caste women experienced more limitations and had fewer freedoms, while some upper-class women had privileges and took part in religious rites.

In ancient China, women had a complicated status that included both opportunities and restrictions. Important was the Confucian ideology, which strongly emphasized male dominance and filial piety. Although it was expected of women to be submissive wives and daughters, strong female figures like Empress Wu Zetian existed throughout Chinese history. Social and economic factors also affected women's status; elite women had greater access to education and cultural activities.

It is crucial to remember that these tales only offer a partial picture of the varied experiences that women had in ancient societies. Within each society, women's status differed according to class, wealth, and cultural norms. It is important to keep in mind that gender roles and expectations have changed dramatically over time as we study the ancient world. Our understanding should take into account the complex and nuanced realities of women's lives in the past.

2.2.Networks for Women's Rights;

The term "Networks for Women's Rights" describes the numerous groups, websites, and online forums devoted to advancing and championing women's empowerment and gender equality. These networks are essential in today's digital age for bringing attention to issues, fostering dialogue, and inspiring people and groups to collaborate on the advancement of women's rights.

These networks give women a platform to share their stories and give voice to their opinions, which is one of their main benefits. Women's rights networks provide a forum for discussion through social media, digital campaigns, and online forums. This allows women from different backgrounds to connect and support one another. This encourages a feeling of unity and solidarity, which helps to dispel isolation and gives people the confidence to speak out against injustice and discrimination.

Women's rights networks also use social media and technology to spread awareness among the general public and reach a larger audience. They make use of these platforms to spread knowledge, inform the public about important matters, and galvanize support for causes pertaining to women's rights. They make it possible for people who might not have access to more conventional forms of activism to participate in the movement and bring about significant change by utilizing the power of online activism.

These networks also serve as hubs for sharing resources, research, and best practices. They work in conjunction with scholars, investigators, and proponents of policy to produce innovative research and analyses, offering fact-based remedies to mitigate gender inequalities. This exchange of knowledge aids in the development of strategies and policies that support gender equality and work to remove structural obstacles that stand in the way of women's rights.

Furthermore, grassroots organizing and advocacy are frequent activities of women's rights networks. To increase awareness and demand concrete action, they actively lobby lawmakers, actively campaign for legislative changes, and take part in public demonstrations. Through the utilization of their combined strength, these networks establish a powerful voice that impacts social and political debates, advocating for laws that support women's rights and opposing cultural practices that maintain gender disparity.

Women's rights networks occasionally go beyond national boundaries to create international coalitions that tackle problems that impact women everywhere. They work together with global organizations, participate in international conferences, and have cross-cultural conversations in order to exchange experiences and develop tactics that will affect women's rights more broadly all over the world.

To sum up, networks for women's rights are essential for fostering a positive atmosphere, elevating the voices of women, and bringing about change. These networks significantly contribute to the advancement of gender equality, the empowerment of women, and the transformation of societies to guarantee equal rights for all through the use of technology, promoting dialogue, and mobilizing resources. Their combined efforts support a global movement aimed at achieving a more equal and welcoming world for women.

2.3 The Diverse Fields in Which Women Have Contributed; Throughout history, women have significantly contributed to a wide range of fields. Here are a handful of instances:

1. Science and Technology: Women scientists, like Marie Curie in physics and chemistry, Rosalind Franklin in molecular biology, Ada Lovelace in computer science, and Grace Hopper in computer programming, have made ground-breaking discoveries and advances in these domains.

2. Medicine and Healthcare: Women have been instrumental in the healthcare industry as researchers and physicians alike. Elizabeth Blackwell became the first female doctor in the United States, and Florence Nightingale is credited as the creator of modern nursing. Women have made significant contributions to medical research, public health campaigns, and the creation of novel drugs and therapies.

3. Literature and Writing: The inventiveness and potent storytelling of female writers have enhanced the literary landscape. Prominent writers who have left a lasting impact on literature include

Toni Morrison, Maya Angelou, Emily Dickinson, Jane Austen, and Virginia Woolf.

4. Arts and Entertainment: Women have achieved great success in a variety of artistic disciplines, such as theater, film, music, painting, and sculpture. In addition to their enormous success, artists such as Beyoncé, Georgia O'Keeffe, Aretha Franklin, Audrey Hepburn, Meryl Streep, and Frida Kahlo have cleared the path for upcoming generations of creators.

5. Business and Entrepreneurship: Women are breaking down barriers in traditionally male-dominated industries by becoming powerful

business leaders and entrepreneurs. In their respective industries, entrepreneurs such as Sheryl Sandberg, Oprah Winfrey, Indra Nooyi, and Estée Lauder have had a big impact.

6. Social Sciences and Activism: Women have made significant contributions to the domains of political science, anthropology, psychology, and sociology by offering their perspectives on societal issues and human behavior. Social activism has also benefited from the contributions of well-known feminist thinkers who have championed human rights and gender equality, including Simone

de Beauvoir, Audre Lorde, Malala Yousafzai, and Angela Davis.

These are but a handful of the many different fields that women have significantly contributed to. Women have played significant roles in shaping our world and have triumphed over many challenges to reach success throughout history.

3.The Expression and Identity of Gender;

Gender expression and identity are intricate subjects that involve a range of factors, such as individual self-perception, cultural norms, societal expectations, and personal experiences. Gender refers to the social and cultural roles, behaviors, and expectations associated with being male or female, whereas sex relates to biological characteristics such as reproductive organs and chromosomes.

Historically, societies have frequently relied on a binary conception of gender, in which people are categorized as male or female according to the sex they were assigned at birth. It is crucial to understand, though, that gender can manifest itself in a variety of ways and is not exclusively based on biology.

Gender expression is the process by which people show others who they are by acting in certain ways, showing their features, and dressing a certain way. These expressions are not restricted to the conventional gender stereotypes and can take many different forms. A person assigned to the gender of a man at birth, for instance, might defy social norms and expectations by expressing their gender through feminine attire and behaviors.

A strong sense of being male, female, or of a different gender that may or may not correspond with the assigned sex at birth is known as gender identity. While some people identify as transgender, non-binary, genderqueer, or with other gender identities outside of the binary, others may identify as the gender that was assigned to them at birth (cisgender). Respecting and validating an individual's self-identified gender is crucial, as it is highly personal and best left to their own determination.

It is also critical to acknowledge that gender is a spectrum and that there are a variety of gender identities and expressions outside of the binary concept. The gender experiences of each individual are unique and deserving of acceptance and respect.

Gender diversity has gained more attention and recognition in recent years, which has resulted in more welcoming environments where people can express their gender identities. Society must never stop encouraging tolerance and acceptance, dispelling false beliefs, and advocating for equality and inclusivity for all people, regardless of gender identity or expression.

3.1 Gender and Sex: Recognizing the Distinction;

The terms gender and sex actually refer to different concepts, despite the fact that they are often interchanged.

Biochemical traits that set males and females apart are referred to as "sex." An individual's reproductive system and genetic makeup usually determine these traits. Based on their sex organs, chromosomes (XX for females, XY for males), and other physical characteristics, people are typically categorized as male or female.

However, gender is a social construct that is shaped by culture and society, and it includes the expectations, roles, and behaviors that are connected to being a certain way. Regardless of one's biological sex, gender identity is the intensely felt sense that one is male, female, or something else.

Contrary to what many societies might imply, gender is not always binary. Transgender, non-binary, and genderqueer are examples of people who identify as something other than the gender that was assigned to them at birth. The range of gender expressions embodied by these identities surpasses conventional concepts of binary thinking.

The fact that gender identity is internal to each individual and that everyone has the freedom to self-identify and express their gender in a way that is true to them should also be understood. A vital component of inclusivity and the advancement of human rights is respecting and recognizing people for who they are, regardless of how they identify their gender.

Recognizing the distinction between gender and sex allows us to better understand and appreciate the complexity of human identity. It supports the development of a more tolerant and inclusive society that values people's right to freely express their gender identity and respects their right to self-determination.

3.2 The Stereotypes of Women and Gender

;Stereotypes of women and gender have been present in societies around the world for centuries. These stereotypes can differ between cultures and geographical areas, and they are frequently founded on social, cultural, and historical norms. Even though it is critical to recognize that not everyone fits into these stereotypes, they nevertheless influence how people perceive and anticipate things.

The notion that men are logical and assertive, and women are sentimental and nurturing, is one prevalent stereotype. According to this stereotype, men should be leaders and decision-makers and women are more likely to take on caring roles like motherhood or childcare. Though there are undoubtedly those who exhibit these attributes, it is crucial to understand that emotional intelligence and nurturing traits are not exclusive to men, and that all genders can possess rationality and assertiveness.

Another stereotype concerns standards of beauty and physical appearance for women. Women's youthfulness, slimness, and physical attractiveness are highly valued qualities in society. This stereotype may cause women to feel under pressure to meet unattainable beauty standards, which can result in problems with body image and low self-esteem. It is critical to support body positivity, affirm that beauty exists in all forms, and recognize that people should not be evaluated only on the basis of their outward appearance.

Stereotypes about careers and professions also support gender inequality. Historically, women have been drawn to professions like teaching or nursing, while men have dominated fields like science, technology, engineering, and mathematics (STEM). These stereotypes restrict women's options and uphold the idea that some occupations are better suited for one gender than another. There has been an attempt to dismantle these barriers based on gender and inspire women and girls to pursue careers in any field they choose.

Furthermore, women's autonomy and capacity for decision-making may be restricted by stereotypes. Women are expected to put their family and household duties ahead of their personal goals in some cultures. This may serve to uphold established gender norms and limit the options available to women regarding their lifestyle, profession, and educational path.

To build a society that is more inclusive and egalitarian, it is imperative that we confront and challenge these stereotypes. Gender stereotypes can be dismantled through education, awareness, and diversity promotion, which emphasize that people should not be classified or evaluated according to their gender. Achieving gender equality requires motivating people to follow their passions, objectives, and dreams regardless of their gender.

3.3 Women Who Are Nonbinary and Transgende;.

The community of women who identify as transgender and nonbinary is vibrant and diverse within the gender spectrum. People whose gender identity does not exclusively fit into the male or female categories are referred to as nonbinary. On the other hand, people who identify as transgender are those whose gender identity does not correspond with the sex assigned to them at birth.

When it comes to navigating gender identity, cultural expectations, and getting access to support networks and healthcare, nonbinary and transgender women frequently confront particular difficulties. Respecting and validating their identities and experiences is crucial, as is recognizing the intersections between gender identity and expression.

Creating welcoming environments, encouraging acceptance, and granting access to resources and healthcare services tailored to their individual needs are all part of supporting nonbinary and transgender women. Important first steps toward inclusivity and support include confirming their gender identity, utilizing appropriate pronouns and names, and comprehending and honoring their range of experiences.

Understanding that nonbinary and transgender women may have very different experiences is crucial. Everybody has a different journey, and it is important to hear about and respect each person's struggles, victories, and stories. Through self-education, confronting our personal prejudices, and promoting parity, we can foster a society that is more welcoming and inclusive to all women, including those who identify as nonbinary and transgender.

4.Women and Intersectionality; The term "women and intersectionality" refers to a perspective that acknowledges the ways in which various intersecting systems of oppression—such as ableism, heterosexism, sexism, racism, classism, and others—have an impact on women's experiences. In order to highlight the ways in which different types of oppression intersect and affect the lives of people who have multiple marginalized identities, legal scholar Kimberlé Crenshaw first introduced the concept of intersectionality in the late 1980s.

Intersectionality, as it pertains to women's experiences, recognizes that discrimination and inequality are more complex than gender. Unique challenges that are inextricably linked to their other social identities confront women from diverse racial, ethnic, socioeconomic, and cultural backgrounds. According to intersectionality, distinct groups of women have distinct experiences and outcomes as a result of these various dimensions of identity interacting and intersecting.

In addition to gender-based discrimination, black women may encounter racism, which can present unique difficulties and experiences that are not always shared by white women. Similarly, obstacles that compound the problems faced by a woman with a disability can be linked to both ableism and sexism.

By highlighting the significance of addressing multiple forms of oppression at once, intersectionality enables a more nuanced analysis of women's experiences. It underscores that, in order to effectively advance justice and social change, gender equality strategies must also take other forms of discrimination into account and address them.

Intersectionality provides a framework for identifying and comprehending the interlocking systems of oppression that affect women's lives. This makes it possible to make efforts toward gender equality more inclusive and equitable for all women, not just those in positions of privilege. In mainstream feminist movements, marginalized women's voices are frequently ignored or undervalued. This highlights the significance of considering diverse perspectives and elevating their voices.

4.1 Women's Experiences, Race, and Ethnicity;

The experiences of women are influenced by a number of variables, such as race and ethnicity. Women face particular challenges and perspectives because of the intersectionality of gender, race, and ethnicity.

Diverse racial and ethnic backgrounds of women frequently experience unique forms of discrimination and oppression. Women of color, for instance, may face both sexism and racism at the same time, which exacerbates their disadvantages. Their access to opportunities for healthcare, work, education, and other services may be hampered by institutional barriers, prejudices, and stereotypes.

Women from various racial and ethnic backgrounds have different experiences depending on historical and cultural contexts. African American women, for example, have experienced systemic sexism and racism due to the laws of Jim Crow, the legacy of slavery, and ongoing racial inequality. The experiences of Latinx women as women may be impacted by challenges associated with immigration, language barriers, and cultural marginalization.

Moreover, cultural norms and expectations differ among various racial and ethnic groups, which affects the expectations and roles that are put on women. A woman's family life, professional and educational choices, and sense of fulfillment can all be impacted by these expectations. Asian American women, for instance, may experience expectations of academic achievement and pressure to adhere to traditional gender norms.

For all women to live in inclusion and equality, it is critical to acknowledge and address these intersecting experiences. In addition to promoting a more inclusive feminist movement that recognizes and works toward the liberation of all women, intersectional feminism aims to address the particular difficulties faced by women from a variety of racial and ethnic backgrounds.

As they contribute a variety of viewpoints and insights to conversations on gender equality, it is imperative to elevate the voices and experiences of women from diverse racial and ethnic backgrounds. We can endeavor to create a more equitable and welcoming society for all by acknowledging, comprehending, and valuing the experiences of women from all racial and ethnic backgrounds.

4.2. Women's Lives and Socioeconomic Factors;

Socioeconomic factors encompass a wide range of elements, including income, education, employment opportunities, access to healthcare and justice systems, social norms, and cultural attitudes.

Income and financial stability are two major socioeconomic factors that have a significant impact on women's lives. Historically, women have been more likely than men to live in poverty and to face large wage gaps. In addition to worsening gender disparities, lower income levels frequently result in restricted access to healthcare, education, and other necessities.

Education access is another important component. The socioeconomic status of women is positively impacted when they have equal access to high-quality education. Women who have an education are more powerful because they have the information, abilities, and self-assurance to question social norms, pursue better job prospects, and participate in decision-making processes. It is also essential in ending the intergenerational cycle of poverty.

The work environment and employment prospects have a big impact on women's lives. Women frequently face challenges such as occupational segregation, gender discrimination, and unequal opportunities for career advancement. Women are disproportionately employed in low-wage, unstable jobs, which hinders their ability to become financially independent and advance in society as a whole.

Reproductive rights and access to healthcare are essential to women's socioeconomic advancement and general well-being. Women's physical and emotional well-being depends on access to quality healthcare services, which includes family planning, reproductive healthcare, and maternal health services. Insufficient availability of these services may result in elevated rates of maternal death, restricted options for family planning, and impaired general health.

Women's experiences are greatly influenced by social norms and cultural beliefs. The socioeconomic indicators of societies that support gender equality, dispel harmful stereotypes, and give women equal opportunities are typically higher. On the other hand, societies that uphold gender-based violence, discriminatory norms, and unequal power relations impede the advancement of women and restrict their socioeconomic opportunities.

In order to address the socioeconomic factors that have an impact on women's lives, policies, legislation, and institutional support are essential. In order to guarantee equitable compensation, encourage inclusive education, establish safe working conditions, and enhance access to social services and healthcare, governments and organizations must put policies into place. Furthermore, attitudes and behaviors can be changed by questioning society norms and advancing gender equality through awareness campaigns and education.

In conclusion, women's lives are influenced by a complex web of socioeconomic factors. A comprehensive strategy that supports equitable access to healthcare, education, decent work, and legal protection is needed to address these factors. Societies have the ability to empower women, improve their well-being, and unleash their full socio-economic potential by tackling these factors and pursuing gender equality.

4.3. Women with Special Needs

;Women who have physical, mental, emotional, or sensory impairments are referred to as having special needs. These women may require additional support or have disabilities. These impairments may be acquired later in life, be congenital, or result from an illness or accident.

Since that discrimination and marginalization against women with special needs can take many different forms, it is critical to recognize and address the particular difficulties these women face. Their chances and rights may be restricted since they frequently face obstacles to social inclusion, work, healthcare, and education.

For women with special needs, having access to education is essential. To fully engage in educational programs, they might need assistive technologies, modifications, or specialized learning support. It is imperative that educational institutions be inclusive, offering equal opportunities and recognizing a range of abilities.

Women with special needs frequently have less work options, which raises the unemployment or underemployment rates. To guarantee that women with special needs have equitable opportunities for professional advancement and financial independence, employers ought to prioritize inclusive hiring practices, reasonable accommodations, accessible work environments, and equal compensation.

Women with special needs may have difficulty obtaining appropriate medical care when it comes to healthcare. It is imperative that healthcare providers provide inclusive care, taking into account the unique needs and accommodations that these women demand. To guarantee their general well-being, it is critical to provide them with respectful treatment, accessible facilities, and communication tools.

One of the most important aspects of meeting the needs of women with disabilities is social inclusion. The goal of society should be to establish an atmosphere devoid of prejudice and open to all. This entails raising public awareness and understanding as well as facilitating accessibility in information, transit, and public areas.

Additionally, women with special needs ought to have access to resources and specialized support services that are catered to their particular situation. This includes advocacy services, peer support groups, counseling, and therapy that can help them overcome obstacles and develop their skills and independence.

In conclusion, it is critical to acknowledge the diversity of women with special needs as a population. Numerous conditions and levels of support are needed for a variety of disabilities, such as physical, mental, and sensory impairments, as well as chronic illnesses and mental health issues.

Through the advancement of inclusivity, the dismantling of obstacles, and the provision of assistance, society can enable women with special needs to lead satisfying lives, accomplish their objectives, and enhance their communities. In order to guarantee equality and opportunity for all, it is imperative to advance and defend their rights.

Of course! Here are some other things to think about when it comes to women with special needs:

1. Sexual and Reproductive Health: Women with special needs may experience particular difficulties in

these areas. To make educated decisions about family planning, pregnancy, contraception, and sexual health, they might need access to readily available information, healthcare services, and support. Healthcare professionals ought to receive training on how to compassionately and impartially attend to their unique needs.

2. Abuse and Violence: Women who require special assistance are more vulnerable to abuse, exploitation, and violence. Because they are dependent on caregivers or have communication barriers, they may find it difficult to identify and report abuse. It is especially important to

give them access to safe spaces, resources, and legal safeguards. Raising awareness and educating women with special needs about their rights and the resources at their disposal is crucial.

3. Mental Health and Well-Being: Women who have special needs may be more susceptible to mental health problems like loneliness, depression, and anxiety. It is crucial that they have access to mental health services and accommodations that take into account their particular needs. Their general well-being can be greatly improved by establishing inclusive settings that encourage social interactions

and by giving them access to recreational opportunities.

4. Intersectionality: It is critical to understand that, in addition to specific forms of discrimination, women with special needs may also experience prejudice on the basis of their race, ethnicity, religion, sexual orientation, or socioeconomic background. When comprehending their experiences and creating all-encompassing strategies to meet their unique needs, intersectionality should be taken into account.

5. Caregiver Support: A lot of women with special needs depend on caregivers for their everyday needs, which can be emotionally and

physically taxing. It is critical to acknowledge the value of caregiver support, resources, relief care, and help in effectively managing caregiving duties. The wellbeing and mental health of caregivers themselves should also receive consideration.

6. Empowerment and Advocacy: It is important to give women with special needs the freedom to fully engage in life-affecting decision-making. In order to guarantee that their needs are systematically met, their rights are upheld, and their voices are heard, advocacy is essential. It is imperative that women with special needs actively participate in the

development of policies, programs, and services that impact them.

In conclusion, comprehensive approaches encompassing social inclusion, work, healthcare, education, and support services are needed to address the needs of women with special needs. Through acknowledging the distinct obstacles these women encounter and striving for inclusive and easily accessible settings, we can advance parity and enable these women to lead satisfying lives.

4.4.LGBTQ+ Women; The greater LGBTQ+ community is enriched by the presence of

LGBTQ+ women. They stand for a wide range of people who identify as non-heterosexual or non-cisgender, lesbian, gay, bisexual, transgender, queer, or in any other way.

LGBTQ+ women encounter particular difficulties and experiences, just like any other LGBTQ+ person. Due to their gender identity or sexual orientation, they may face prejudice, discrimination, and social stigma. As LGBTQ+ women may experience additional discrimination based on factors like race, ethnicity, religion, ability, or socioeconomic status, they may also run into intersectional issues.

Notwithstanding these obstacles, LGBTQ+ women have made noteworthy advances in activism, culture, and society. They have been instrumental in pushing for greater equality and the advancement of LGBTQ+ rights. Prominent LGBTQ+ women have influenced and enhanced our collective experience in a variety of fields, including politics, music, literature, and the arts.

In addition, LGBTQ+ women have established networks of support and community to give each other a sense of empowerment, understanding, and belonging. Diverse identities, experiences, and relationships can be celebrated in these settings. Events and organizations supporting LGBTQ+ women, like Pride marches and women's LGBTQ+ conferences, offer forums for networking, education, and visibility.

In order to support LGBTQ+ women's rights and well-being, it is critical to acknowledge the distinctive experiences and difficulties they face.

1. Intersectionality: Discrimination and marginalization against LGBTQ+ women frequently take intersecting forms. Factors like age, immigration status, disability, race, ethnicity, and religion can influence their experiences. It is essential to

acknowledge and address these intersecting identities in order to comprehend the intricacies and particular requirements of LGBTQ+ women.

2. Health and wellbeing: Women who identify as LGBTQ+ may face particular health issues and inequalities. They frequently have particular healthcare requirements, such as having access to services for reproductive health, care that is gender affirming, and mental health support. Healthcare systems that are inclusive, culturally sensitive, and take into account the varied experiences of LGBTQ+ women are necessary to address these problems.

3. Families and relationships: Same-sex partnerships, marriages, cohabitation, and parenthood are just a few examples of the diverse families and relationships that LGBTQ+ women form. In order to obtain rights and recognition for their relationships and families, they might run into social and legal obstacles. It is imperative for LGBTQ+ women to advocate for inclusive legal frameworks and policies to guarantee their ability to establish and preserve satisfying and safe family structures.

4. Transgender women: In the community of LGBTQ+ women, transgender women are entitled to

special consideration. women are people who identify as women but were born with a male gender assignment. They face particular difficulties getting healthcare, legal recognition, social acceptance, and affirmation of their gender identity. Promoting inclusivity and equality requires defending the rights and welfare of transgender women.

5. Representation and visibility: In order to dispel prejudice and foster acceptance, LGBTQ+ women's representation and visibility in the media, in politics, and in other public domains are essential. Understanding, empathy, and empowerment are fostered by supporting varied representations of

LGBTQ+ women, their experiences, and their contributions.

6. Allies and support: To advance equality and inclusion for LGBTQ+ women, forging alliances across communities is crucial. Allies can help LGBTQ+ women by educating themselves, speaking out against prejudice, fighting for equal rights, and establishing safe spaces where everyone is valued and respected. Allies can support LGBTQ+ women both inside and outside of the LGBTQ+ community.

It is essential to recognize and celebrate the diversity within the LGBTQ+ women's community in order to break down barriers, promote inclusivity, and advance equality for all people, regardless of their gender identity or sexual orientation. Through collaboration, we can establish a community that honors and cherishes the diversity of LGBTQ+ women's experiences and accomplishments.

5. Empowerment and Rights of Women; The establishment of a fair and equitable society depends on the rights and empowerment of women. The ability of women to realize their full potential, take part in decision-making, and be in charge of their own lives is referred to as women's empowerment. Empowerment on all fronts—social, economic, political, and cultural—is included.

One of the cornerstones of human rights and fundamental human dignity is the equality of women. Women ought to enjoy equal rights and protections under the law, as well as equal opportunities in the fields of healthcare, work, and education. In order to achieve gender equality, discriminatory attitudes, laws, and practices that restrict women's rights and opportunities must be opposed and changed.

The following are some essential facets of women's rights and empowerment:

1. Education: It is imperative to guarantee girls' and women's access to high-quality education. Through knowledge, skills, and chances for both professional and personal growth, education empowers women. It enhances health outcomes, advances gender equality,

and aids in ending the cycle of poverty.

2. Economic empowerment: Women ought to have equal access to financial independence and economic participation. This entails getting equitable pay, granting access to resources, credit, and employment opportunities, as well as doing away with discrimination against women in the workplace.

3. Political involvement: It is imperative that women take an active role in politics and decision-making. Increasing the number of women in elected offices and other leadership roles—including local councils,

cabinets, and legislatures—is imperative. The opinions and voices of women are vital in forming laws and policies that impact them.

4. Health and wellbeing: Women should have access to all medical services, including family planning, maternity care, and reproductive health. It is imperative to put an end to gender-based violence, which encompasses sexual assault, domestic abuse, and human trafficking, in order to protect women's safety and wellbeing.

5. Social and cultural norms: It is critical to question damaging social and cultural norms that support gender inequality. This entails

dispelling gender stereotypes, elevating positive role models, and fostering an environment that is welcoming and inclusive while honoring the contributions and rights of women.

To advance and defend women's rights and empowerment, it is critical that individuals, groups, governments, and communities collaborate. Through this approach, it is possible to establish a just and balanced community in which each woman can reach her maximum potential and prosper.

6.Women Writers and Authors;

Women authors and writers have contributed significantly to literature throughout history by presenting a variety of viewpoints and narrative modalities. In addition to providing readers with entertainment, their works have influenced social and cultural contexts. A handful of well-known female writers and authors are as follows:

1. Jane Austen: Known for her brilliant storytelling and witty social commentary, Austen is a celebrated author. Her books, which include "Pride and Prejudice" and "Emma," examine women's lives in

eighteenth-century England and emphasize their battles for autonomy and love.

2. Virginia Woolf: Known for her inventive storytelling methods, Woolf was a prominent modernist writer. She is regarded as a pioneer of feminist literature for her exploration of gender, identity, and mental health in works like "Mrs. Dalloway" and "To the Lighthouse."

3. Toni Morrison: A trailblazing African American author, Morrison delves into intricate matters of race, identity, and the past. Her Pulitzer Prize-winning book "Beloved" explores the legacy of slavery and

how it affects both individuals and communities.

4. Harper Lee: In the 1930s, racial injustice and social injustice in the Deep South were topics covered in Lee's well-known book "To Kill a Mockingbird." The book, which has gone on to become a classic, emphasizes the ability of storytelling to spark change.

5. Maya Angelou: The renowned poet, memoirist, and civil rights advocate was well-known. Her autobiography, "I Know Why the Caged Bird Sings," has been praised for its honesty and resiliency as it documents her experiences growing up as a Black woman in America.

6. Chimamanda Ngozi Adichie: Nigerian novelist Adichie is well-known for her compelling stories and exploration of feminism and post-colonialism. Her books, which include "Americanah" and "Half of a Yellow Sun," explore issues of race, identity, and cross-cultural conflicts.

7. J.K. Rowling: Her "Harry Potter" series, which went on to become an international sensation, captivated the minds of millions of people. Her writings provided readers with entertainment value while imparting wisdom on friendship, bravery, and overcoming adversity.

These are but a handful of the many female writers and authors who have made a lasting impression on the literary community. Readers of all backgrounds continue to be inspired, challenged, and engaged by their works. Women writers are essential to the canon of literature because they offer unique perspectives and compelling narratives.

8. Mary Shelley: At the age of just 21, Shelley wrote the novel "Frankenstein," which is what made her most famous. This Gothic masterpiece is a classic in the science fiction and horror genres, delving into themes of creation, ambition, and the human condition.

9. Louisa May Alcott: The Civil War-era lives of four sisters are portrayed in this well-loved classic, "Little Women," by Alcott. The book has influenced readers for many years to come as it delves into themes of female autonomy, love, and family.

10.Emily Dickinson: Mostly unpublished during her lifetime, Dickinson's poetry is recognized for its poignancy and introspection. Her poems, which explore themes of nature, love, death, and the human spirit, highlight her distinct and intensely personal voice.

11. Sylvia Plath: Known for her honest and intensely felt writing, Plath was a significant poet and novelist. Her semi-autobiographical novel "The Bell Jar" chronicles a young woman's battle with mental illness, and her hauntingly intense poetry, including "Daddy" and "Lady Lazarus," is well known.

12. Zora Neale Hurston: Hurston was an anthropologist and writer who was well-known during the Harlem Renaissance. Her book "Their Eyes Were Watching God" captures the experiences of African American women in the early 20th century while examining themes of love, self-discovery, and racial identity.

13. Arundhati Roy: Roy, an Indian writer, became well-known throughout the world for her book "The God of Small Things," which is a poetic and moving account of love, family, and social constraints that is set in Kerala, India. Since then, she has developed into an outspoken activist for a range of political and social causes.

14. Margaret Atwood: Known for her feminist themes and speculative fiction, Atwood is a Canadian author. Her book "The Handmaid's Tale" explores themes of oppression, gender, and power in a dystopian future where women's rights are severely curtailed.

15. Isabella Allende: Known for her vividly imaginative storytelling, Allende is a Chilean-American writer. Her works, which include "The House of the Spirits" and "Eva Luna," combine elements of magic realism with compelling stories that delve into the themes of family, politics, and love.

These female writers and authors have made a variety of important, thought-provoking, and varied contributions to the literary community. Readers are still struck by their experiences and viewpoints, which encourages empathy, comprehension, and respect for the experiences of women.

7. Healthcare and Welfare of Women;

The welfare and health of women are essential to the advancement and well-being of any society. It covers a wide range of topics, such as women's economic empowerment, access to high-quality healthcare services, rights related to reproductive health, and the prevention and support of gender-based violence.

Making sure women have access to comprehensive and reasonably priced healthcare services is a major area of focus. This covers family planning, prenatal and postnatal care, and regular screenings for diseases like breast and cervical cancer, among other reproductive health services. It is also crucial for women to have access to safe abortion services and contraception because these options empower them to make decisions about their reproductive lives and promote their general health.

Another essential element of advancing women's healthcare and welfare is addressing gender-based violence. Women are frequently the targets of violence, including sexual assault, domestic abuse, and human trafficking. In order to provide safe spaces for women, increase public awareness of these issues, offer legal protection, and assist victims of violence, governments and communities should collaborate.

Encouraging women's economic empowerment is essential for their general welfare as well. Equal access to education, employment opportunities, and pay is a fundamental right for women. Women should be able to pursue their careers and take care of their families by having policies in place to address workplace discrimination and maintain work-life balance. Initiatives like microfinance programs can also assist women in launching their own businesses and achieving financial independence.

Fair access to healthcare services requires funding healthcare and social programs that are especially designed for marginalized groups, such as low-income women, members of minority groups, and refugees. These programs ought to address the particular difficulties that these groups encounter and offer specialized assistance to successfully meet their needs.

Furthermore, advancing the welfare and health of women depends on comprehensive sex education in schools. It assists young boys and girls in forming healthy relationships, understanding their bodies, and making decisions regarding their reproductive health. Society can promote more positive views about women's bodies and sexuality by dispelling the stigma and taboos associated with these subjects.

All things considered, a comprehensive strategy is needed to guarantee the health and welfare of women. Collaboration among governments, civil society organizations, healthcare providers, and communities is imperative in addressing the multifaceted needs of women, advancing gender equality, and championing their rights and overall well-being in all spheres of life.

7.1.Health of Women's Body;

A woman's total well-being is greatly influenced by the state of her body. Women's physical, mental, and reproductive health are among the many aspects that go into keeping them in good health.

1. Physical well-being: Consistent exercise, a healthy diet rich in balance, enough sleep, and abstaining from bad habits (like smoking or binge drinking) are all important for women's physical well-being. Consulting with medical professionals on a regular basis can assist in identifying possible problems early on.

2. Mental health: Good mental health is a prerequisite for good physical health. Mental health issues like stress, anxiety, and depression are more common in women. Developing healthy coping strategies, taking part in enjoyable and relaxing activities, getting support when needed, and practicing self-care are all important aspects of maintaining mental health.

3. Reproductive health: This encompasses menopause, pregnancy, contraception, and menstruation. Reproductive health depends on getting regular gynecological exams, practicing

good hygiene during menstruation, using contraception safely and effectively, and getting appropriate medical advice when pregnant.

4. Preventive screenings: It is advised that women get regular screenings for conditions like osteoporosis, cervical cancer, and breast cancer, such as Pap smears and mammograms. These examinations aid in the early identification and management of possible health problems.

5. Knowledge of common health issues: Women need to be informed about particular health issues like osteoporosis, heart disease, ovarian and breast cancer, and hormone

imbalances. Maintaining optimal health can be aided by knowledge of the risk factors, symptoms, and preventative techniques associated with these conditions.

Women should put their health first by adopting healthy lifestyle practices, going to the doctor when necessary, and taking the initiative to get preventive care. Maintaining regular contact with medical professionals can help guarantee a woman's general health and well-being and offer tailored advice based on her unique needs.

7.2.Intimate Partner Abuse and Violence

;Any pattern of behavior used by one person to exercise dominance and control over their intimate partner is referred to as intimate partner abuse and violence. Financial, emotional, sexual, or physical abuse are just a few of the ways it can appear. All genders, sexual orientations, and types of relationships are impacted by this issue.

Physical abuse refers to the application of force—such as striking, slapping, choking, or using weapons—that results in harm or injury. Any coercion, assault, or non-consensual sexual activity that occurs in a relationship is considered sexual abuse. Behaviors that cause someone to lose confidence in themselves, control their emotions, separate them from friends and family, or undermine their self-worth are all considered forms of emotional abuse.

Financial abuse includes restricting an intimate partner's access to money, controlling or manipulating their financial resources, or taking advantage of their dependence on money. Intimate partner violence and abuse are rarely isolated incidents; instead, they are frequently marked by a pattern of escalating behavior.

It is critical to understand that violence and abuse against intimate partners can take many forms beyond physical acts; emotional and psychological abuse can have just as disastrous consequences on an individual's health. Numerous medical and psychological issues, such as physical harm, persistent pain, anxiety, depression, low self-esteem, and post-traumatic stress disorder (PTSD), can affect victims.

Intimate partner abuse and violence necessitates a multifaceted response from individuals, groups, and organizations. The main goals of prevention should be to upend cultural norms that support violence, encourage healthy relationships, and educate the public.

Support services—like hotlines, counseling, and shelters—are essential in helping survivors because they offer them resources, safety, and emotional support. If necessary, they can also help them navigate the legal system. Establishing a culture that supports survivors, encourages speaking out against abuse, and holds offenders accountable for their actions is crucial.

Seeking support and assistance is crucial if you or someone you know is a victim of violence or abuse by an intimate partner. Speak with authorities, local groups, or hotlines to discuss your circumstances and find out what resources are available. Never forget that there are people out there who can support and help you; you are not alone.

Of course! Apart from the direct effects on the individuals concerned, intimate partner abuse and violence also have extensive ramifications for families, communities, and the broader society. Children who see or witness intimate partner violence are more likely to experience behavioral and emotional issues, which can have a long-term detrimental effect on their physical and mental health.

Intervention strategies that target victims as well as offenders should be part of any effort to address intimate partner abuse and violence. It is essential to give survivors all the support they need, including financial resources, counseling services, safe housing, and legal support. It is crucial to give survivors the tools they need to take back control of their lives and to plan for their safety and wellbeing.

Holding those who commit crimes responsible for their actions is equally crucial. This entails offering intervention programs that target the core causes of violence, alter abusive behaviors, and foster more positive relationship dynamics.

Additionally essential to ending the cycle of abuse and assisting offenders in creating peaceful coping mechanisms are rehabilitation programs.

It takes a team effort to prevent violence and abuse against intimate partners. In order to advance gender equality, consent, healthy relationships, and conflict resolution abilities, education and awareness campaigns should be launched. Age-appropriate education on healthy relationships should be incorporated into the programs offered by schools, community organizations, and healthcare providers.

It is crucial to question cultural norms that support violence, such as toxic masculinity and victim-blaming beliefs. Men's conversations about empathy, respect, and masculinity can change the narrative and foster an inclusive and polite society.

Intimate partner abuse and violence must be recognized and criminalized by law in order to provide survivors with legal protections and offenders with penalties. Laws ought to be made stronger and more strictly enforced, and legal systems ought to take survivors' particular difficulties into consideration.

In the end, eliminating violence and abuse against intimate partners necessitates a multifaceted strategy that includes social change, prevention, support for victims, and treatment for offenders. To build a safer and more just society, it is a complicated issue that calls for constant dedication and cooperation from individuals, communities, organizations, and legislators.

7.3.Health Disparities and Intersectionality;

Health disparities are variations between various groups of people in terms of health outcomes or access to healthcare. Numerous factors, such as socioeconomic status, race/ethnicity, gender, age, and geographic location, can have an impact on these disparities.

The concept of intersectionality acknowledges the interdependence of oppressive systems and social identities. It implies that people's multiple social identities—race, gender, class, and sexual orientation—may overlap, resulting in overlapping forms of discrimination and disadvantage.

People who belong to multiple marginalized groups may experience compounded health inequalities when examining health disparities through an intersectional lens. For instance, due to both racial and socioeconomic factors, a black woman from a low-income background may face disparities in accessing healthcare.

The concept of intersectionality emphasizes how crucial it is to acknowledge the distinct needs and experiences of people who straddle several identities. It highlights the necessity of more thorough and individualized methods to address health disparities. Policymakers, healthcare professionals, and researchers can create interventions and policies that more effectively address the needs of marginalized populations and advance health equity by having a better understanding of the intersections between various forms of discrimination.

Intersectionality also highlights the significance of gathering and analyzing data according to various social identities. Through an analysis of health outcomes and care access across multiple intersecting categories, specific areas of disparity can be identified, and targeted solutions can be developed.

A comprehensive strategy that takes intersectionality into account is needed to address health disparities and promote health equity. In order to guarantee that everyone has an equal chance to lead healthy lives, regardless of how their intersecting identities are expressed, it entails addressing systemic barriers and advancing social justice. Policies that address the social determinants of health, broaden access to high-quality healthcare, lessen prejudice and discrimination in healthcare settings, and elevate the voices of underrepresented groups in decision-making processes can all help achieve this.

8. Problems and Difficulties That Today's Women Face;

Despite great advancements in gender equality, women still confront a variety of issues and challenges today. The following are some of the main obstacles that women in modern society must overcome:

1. Gender-Based Violence: Human trafficking, sexual harassment, assault, and domestic abuse are just a few of the many instances of gender-based violence that still affect women. These actions not only have grave immediate repercussions but also cause emotional and psychological damage that takes time to heal.

2. Unequal Pay and Employment Opportunities: Women are frequently subjected to pay discrimination, with lower pay received for equivalent work performed by men. Women also frequently experience barriers to career advancement and are underrepresented in leadership positions. They are unable to perform to the best of their abilities at work because of this glass ceiling.

3. Inadequate Support for Maternity and Childcare: Women frequently shoulder the responsibility of juggling work and family obligations. Due to a lack of accessible and affordable childcare,

cultural expectations, and insufficient maternity leave, women are frequently forced to choose between their family's needs and their professional goals.

4. Lack of Reproductive Rights and Healthcare: Some women face challenges and obstacles when attempting to obtain reproductive healthcare, such as access to comprehensive sexual education, abortion services, and contraception. Women's autonomy and capacity to make knowledgeable decisions about their bodies may be hampered by these restrictions.

5. Gender Stereotypes and Societal Pressures: Women are subject to

stereotypes and expectations from society about their roles, behavior, and outward appearance. These misconceptions have the power to restrict women's options, uphold established gender norms, and support prejudice and discrimination.

6. Limited Political Representation: Women continue to be underrepresented in positions of political leadership worldwide, notwithstanding advancements. The absence of representation hinders the progress of gender-equality initiatives and denies policymakers the opportunity to consider a variety of viewpoints.

7. Cyberbullying and Online Harassment: As social media and other digital communication platforms have grown in popularity, there has been an increase in cyberbullying and online harassment directed at women. Serious repercussions from this cyber misogyny may include dangers to one's personal safety, harm to one's reputation, and psychological distress.

8. Lack of Access to Education: Despite tremendous advancements toward gender parity in education, some areas continue to deny girls their right to a high-quality education. Women's empowerment, economic opportunities, and

capacity to fully engage in society
are impeded by limited access to
education.

It is critical to address these issues
as a group by enacting new
legislation, raising social awareness,
and making proactive efforts to
advance gender equality. We can
build a more equal and inclusive
society for all women if we take this
action.

9.Global Empowerment of Women;

Achieving gender equality, advancing sustainable development, and building a more just and equitable world depend on the global empowerment of women. It is a complex idea that includes a range of ideas, such as political, social, economic, and cultural empowerment.

Ensuring equal access to education is an important part of global women's empowerment. Education gives women the knowledge, abilities, and self-assurance they need to fully engage in society, which has a transformative effect on their empowerment. Unfortunately, due to issues like poverty, cultural norms, and gender discrimination, women and girls still face obstacles in many parts of the world when trying to access education. These obstacles need to be removed, secure learning environments need to be offered, and gender-sensitive educational practices need to be supported.

Another essential component of global women's empowerment is economic empowerment. Equal opportunities should be provided for women to engage in the economy, find respectable employment, and become financially independent. In order to achieve this, it is necessary to address discriminatory practices, guarantee equal pay for equal labor, encourage female entrepreneurship, and give them access to resources, markets, and credit. Supportive laws that provide flexible work schedules, inexpensive child care, and increased representation of women in leadership roles can also help women become more economically empowered.

In order for women to participate in the decision-making processes that impact their lives, they must be politically empowered. This means boosting female leadership, expanding women's involvement in political institutions, and removing structural obstacles that prevent women from holding elected office.

Women's political empowerment can be aided by affirmative action programs, gender-responsive legislation, and electoral reforms.

In order to empower women culturally and socially, negative gender norms, stereotypes, and attitudes that support discrimination and inequality against women must be challenged. This entails advocating for laws, policies, and social norms that are sensitive to gender and protect the equality, dignity, and rights of women. It also entails opposing patriarchal power structures that uphold inequality and enlisting men and boys as allies in the fight for women's empowerment.

Other intersecting forms of discrimination and disadvantage, such as those based on race, ethnicity, religion, disability, or sexual orientation, should be addressed as part of global efforts to empower women. In order to guarantee that women from marginalized groups and varied backgrounds participate in empowerment programs and reap the benefits fairly, intersectional approaches are essential.

Collaboration and partnerships between governments, civil society organizations, and international bodies are essential to achieving global women's empowerment.

Gender equality and women's empowerment must be incorporated into all development agendas and sectors. Women's rights and empowerment should be given priority in programs related to peacebuilding, economic development, healthcare, education, and the environment.

In addition to being important for justice and human rights, global women's empowerment is also crucial for accomplishing sustainable development objectives, lowering poverty, and advancing social progress. We can use women's potential, abilities, and contributions to create a more equitable, prosperous, and inclusive world if we empower them on a global scale.

Addressing the unique obstacles that women in various parts of the world face is essential to advancing the global empowerment of women. This necessitates a sophisticated comprehension of regional contexts, customs, and legal systems. To effectively address the unique obstacles and injustices that women encounter in each community, efforts must be customized.

Women's empowerment is still severely hampered by gender-based violence in many parts of the world. This covers things like sexual harassment, domestic abuse, damaging customs, and human trafficking. Comprehensive tactics are needed to combat gender-based violence, such as awareness campaigns, legal reforms, support services for survivors, and a shift in society perceptions of gender norms.

Another essential component of women's empowerment is having access to healthcare. Equal access to high-quality healthcare, including prenatal care, maternal healthcare, and reproductive health services, should be granted to women. In order to do this, it is necessary to close gaps in the healthcare system, lower the rate of maternal death, guarantee access to contraceptives, and support thorough sexuality education.

A new issue in the global empowerment of women is the digital divide. Digital literacy and access to technology are prerequisites for social and economic empowerment in the modern digital age. Women should have equal access to and use of information and communication technologies, and efforts should be made to close the digital gap.

Facilitating women's involvement in peacebuilding and conflict resolution procedures is essential for enhancing their agency. Since women are frequently disproportionately impacted by armed conflicts, lasting peace and security depend on their meaningful involvement in peace processes. In areas affected by conflict, it is critical to acknowledge and support the role that women play as change agents.

Emphasizing the role of boys and men in advancing women's empowerment is crucial. Establishing a more gender-equal society can be facilitated by interacting with men and questioning damaging norms of masculinity. Initiatives aimed at educating and raising awareness among men and boys have the potential to undermine patriarchal systems and promote gender parity.

In summary, the process of empowering women worldwide is intricate and multidimensional, requiring teamwork and all-encompassing efforts. Ensuring women's rights and equality is not the only important goal; it is also a critical step in the direction of sustainable development, peace, and justice. We can unleash women's full potential, advance inclusive societies, and build a better future for all by empowering women globally.

Many organizations around the world strive to improve the rights and welfare of women. Some well-known groups working to address women's issues globally are listed below:

1. UN Women: Working toward women's rights and full participation in the political, social, and economic spheres, UN Women is the United Nations organization for gender equality and women's empowerment.

2. Global Fund for Women: This group focuses on issues like gender-based violence, economic empowerment, and political participation and provides funding and support to women-led initiatives worldwide.

3. Women's World Banking: Committed to giving low-income women greater access to financial services, this organization promotes gender-inclusive financial systems, provides financial products, and conducts capacity-building initiatives.

4. Equality Now: This global human rights group works to advance the legal rights of women and girls while opposing harmful practices. Their areas of focus include reproductive rights, human trafficking, and sexual violence.

5. Global Plan: Plan International is a child rights organization that

considers gender equality to be extremely important. It aims to make girls' lives better by giving them access to health care, education, and protection from violence. In more than 75 countries, they advocate for girls' rights.

6.The Global Women's Institute is an organization that is based at George Washington University and concentrates on research, understanding-building, and policy advocacy related to gender equity, economic empowerment, and violence against women.

7.Association for Women's Rights in Development (AWID): AWID is a global feminist group that provides research, advocacy, and capacity-building initiatives to groups and activists for women's rights.

8. The International Women's Health Coalition (IWHC) works to promote women's rights to reproductive autonomy and health on a global scale. Their main priorities are promoting policies, aiding neighborhood groups, and encouraging long-lasting transformation.

9. Women Deliver is an international advocacy group that seeks to enhance the rights, health, and general wellbeing of women and girls across the globe. Maternal

health and gender-based violence are among the topics they address.

10. Girls Not Brides: This international alliance works to safeguard girls' rights and provide them with empowerment while also working to end child marriage. To solve the underlying causes and effects of child marriage, they collaborate with groups, governments, and local communities.

In addition to many others, these groups are essential in advancing gender equality, women's rights, and empowerment on a global basis.

Indeed! Here are a few more groups that put forth endless effort to improve women's rights and welfare across the globe:

11. The Women's International League for Peace and Freedom (WILPF) is a group dedicated to bringing about gender justice and peace. Their efforts are directed towards averting conflicts, supporting disarmament, and encouraging women's involvement in peace negotiations.

12. The Girls' Education Initiative of Ghana (GEIG): The goal of GEIG is to guarantee that girls in Ghana receive an education. They break down barriers between genders in

education and empower girls by offering scholarships, mentoring programs, and grassroots advocacy.

13. The Digital Impact Alliance (DIAL) is a nonprofit organization that advocates for digital inclusion, especially for women and girls in developing nations. Their goal is to utilize technology to create opportunities and close the gender gap in the digital sphere.

14. Women's Refugee Commission: This group fights for the rights and welfare of young people, women, and children who have been forcibly displaced. In humanitarian contexts, they support gender equality and offer safety and aid.

15. International Center for Research on Women (ICRW): ICRW works to address gender inequality globally by conducting advocacy and research. They address problems like violence against women, health, education, and economic empowerment.

16. Women in International Security (WIIS): WIIS is an international network that encourages women to take on leadership roles and engage in peace and security-related fields. To help women advance in their careers, they offer networking opportunities, mentorship, and training.

17. Women for Women International: This organization offers economic opportunities, vocational training, awareness of their rights, and access to necessary resources to support marginalized women who have survived war and conflict.

18. International Women's Development Agency (IWDA): IWDA works to promote gender equality and women's leadership throughout the Asia Pacific area. Their areas of focus include women's rights advocacy, addressing violence against women, and economic empowerment of women.

19.Women's Earth Alliance: Offering leadership development, resources, and capacity-building initiatives to tackle environmental justice and climate change, Women's Earth Alliance is committed to empowering women and girls in environmental sustainability.

20. African Women's Development Fund (AWDF): AWDF provides grants, capacity-building, and networking support to women's rights organizations and initiatives throughout Africa. Their areas of focus include ending violence against women, promoting political participation, and empowering the economy.

These and numerous other organizations are essential to the global advancement of women's rights, gender equality, and female empowerment. Their work tackles a range of topics, including leadership, economic empowerment, health, education, and the eradication of gender-based violence.

9.2. Goals for Sustainable Development and Women;

The Sustainable Development Goals (SDGs) are a group of 17 international objectives that the United Nations (UN) set out to address pressing issues like gender inequality, poverty, inequality, and climate change in order to create a sustainable future for all. The SDGs emphasize women's inclusion, empowerment, and rights as major goals in recognition of the critical role that women play in attaining sustainable development. The following are some particular objectives for women-focused sustainable development:

1. Gender Equality (SDG 5): The purpose of this goal is to empower all women and girls and to attain gender equality. It tackles topics like guaranteeing economic empowerment, ensuring equal access to healthcare and education, putting an end to violence and discrimination against women, and

boosting women's involvement in decision-making.

2. Quality Education (SDG 4): The objective of this goal is to provide inclusive, high-quality education to all people, including women and girls. It aims to close the gender gap in education and increase access to opportunities for career training, lifelong learning, and skill development.

3. Good Health and Well-Being (SDG 3): This goal aims to improve the health of women by guaranteeing that they have access to healthcare services related to reproduction and motherhood, lowering the rate of maternal

mortality, treating and preventing non-communicable diseases, advancing their right to sexual orientation and reproduction, and combating gender-based violence.

4. Decent Work and Economic Growth (SDG 8): The objective of this goal is to advance productive employment, inclusive and sustainable economic growth, and decent work for all people, including women. It places a strong emphasis on fair compensation for equal labor, secure, nondiscriminatory workplaces, and easy access to financial services and business opportunities.

5. Climate Action (SDG 13): This goal focuses on the pressing need to reduce greenhouse gas emissions and their effects. Women are crucial to climate resilience and adaptation because they frequently suffer the most from climate-related disasters. For long-term, practical solutions, women's participation in climate action initiatives must be strengthened.

6. Peace, Justice, and Strong Institutions (SDG 16): This goal asks for fostering inclusive and peaceful societies, guaranteeing that everyone has access to justice, and erecting inclusive, capable, and peaceful institutions. The significance of women's involvement

in decision-making procedures and the eradication of discrimination and violence based on gender is acknowledged.

7. Fair Climate and Clean Energy (SDG 7): Making affordable, dependable, sustainable, and contemporary energy available to everyone is the main objective of this goal. The socioeconomic development of women can be impeded by the difficulties they encounter in obtaining clean energy resources. In the energy sector, advocating for gender-responsive policies and initiatives can empower women, enhance their standard of living, and advance climate justice.

8. SDG 2: Ending hunger, achieving food security, enhancing nutrition, and advancing sustainable agricultural methods are the objectives of this goal. In rural areas especially, women are particularly important to agriculture and food production. Sustainable agricultural practices, poverty reduction, and increased food security can all be achieved through empowering women farmers, protecting their land rights, and giving them access to resources and technology.

9. Water and Sanitation (SDG 6): The objective of this goal is to guarantee that everyone has access to inexpensive, safe drinking water as well as sanitation and hygiene.

The task of fetching water is frequently assigned to women and girls, which has an impact on their economic prospects, health, and educational prospects. Gender equality, general well-being, and the provision of better water and sanitation services can all be advanced by involving women in water management, sanitation projects, and decision-making processes.

10. Reduced Inequalities (SDG 10): This goal aims to address the growing differences between and within nations. Discrimination and marginalization against women take many different forms that overlap. It is possible to end gender-based

disparities, empower women, and build more just and equitable societies by promoting equality, social inclusion, and anti-discrimination policies.

11.Sustainable Goal (SDG) is to create human settlements and cities that are safe, resilient, inclusive, and sustainable. In cities, housing, transportation, infrastructure, and public spaces are among the many obstacles that women must overcome. Encouraging inclusive and participatory urban development, addressing gender-responsive urban planning, and enhancing women's safety and mobility can all improve women's well-being and support sustainable urbanization.

DurableThe accomplishment of all the SDGs and the creation of a more just, equitable, and sustainable world depend on gender equality, women's empowerment, and the advancement of women's rights.

9.3 Women's Empowerment and Education;

Education and women's empowerment are closely related because it is essential to women's empowerment and their ability to realize their full potential. Having access to high-quality education for women can have a lot of positive effects that help not just the individual women but also the families, communities, and societies at large.

Women are empowered by education because it gives them opportunities, knowledge, and skills. It provides individuals with the means to exercise their rights, make educated decisions, and engage fully in the social, political, and economic spheres. Women may overcome discrimination, overcome stereotypes and conventional gender roles, and improve their communities by pursuing education.

Women's empowerment and education intersect in several significant ways:

1.   Economic   empowerment:
Education can improve women's
chances of finding employment and
becoming   more   independent
financially. Through the acquisition
of skills and knowledge, women can
take   advantage   of   improved
employment opportunities, launch
or grow businesses, and support
local economies.

2. Health and wellbeing: Increasing
women's access to education is
essential to improving their health
outcomes.   Higher   education
increases a woman's chances of
adopting healthier habits, having
better access to healthcare services,
and making informed decisions

about her reproductive health. Moreover, educated women typically have healthier families because they are more conscious of proper diet, hygiene, and child care techniques.

3. Active participation in social and political spheres: Women who have received education are better able to play these roles. Women with higher levels of education are also more likely to take part in community development projects, fight for their rights and other people's rights, and speak up when decisions are being made at different levels.

4. Gender equity: In order to address gender disparities,

education is essential. Equal access to education for women and girls contributes to the challenge of societal norms that support gender inequality and discrimination. With education, girls and women can take on obstacles, assert their rights, and work toward creating more inclusive communities—all of which advance gender equality.

5. Ending the poverty cycle: One effective way to end the poverty cycle is through education. Women who have an education are better able to support their families and themselves. Better child health and nutrition outcomes, smaller families, and a greater propensity to invest in their own children's

education are all associated with educated women, which feeds a positive cycle of empowerment and development.

Addressing the obstacles that prevent girls and women from obtaining high-quality education is crucial to achieving women's empowerment through education. These obstacles may consist of lack of infrastructure, discriminatory practices, poverty, cultural norms, and violence against women. In order to guarantee equal opportunities for women and girls, measures should be taken, such as establishing policies that promote girls' education, removing gender biases from curricula and teaching materials, and offering accessible and secure educational settings.

6. Leadership and decision-making: Education gives women the information, abilities, and self-assurance they need to assume leadership positions and actively engage in the decision-making process. The views and experiences of women in leadership roles across a range of industries can influence programs and policies that cater to the needs and interests of the general public.

7. Decrease in child marriage and gender-based violence: Education serves as a barrier to reduce both of these issues. Girls who attend school

have a lower chance of being married off at a young age and are better able to understand and stand up for their rights. Another important tool in the fight against cultural norms that support violence against women is education.

8. Climate change resilience: Women are frequently disproportionately affected by climate change. Women who receive an education are better able to adapt to environmental challenges, adopt sustainable practices, and help create communities that are resilient. Women become more capable of addressing climate change and advancing sustainable

development when we provide them with education.

9. Education for peacebuilding and conflict resolution: By encouraging tolerance, comprehension, and communication, education helps to promote peace. Women can make a big difference in preventing violence, resolving conflicts, and fostering peace when they have access to education. The likelihood of educated women advocating for social cohesion and peaceful solutions within their communities is higher.

10. Innovation and technological advancement: Encouraging women to become empowered through

education is essential to advancing both of these areas. Women can contribute to discoveries and advances in a variety of fields when they receive education and empowerment in STEM (science, technology, engineering, and mathematics). Gender parity is promoted in these historically male-dominated fields by supporting girls' education in STEM.

11. Impact on future generations: Empowering women via education has a positive ripple effect on other generations. Higher educational attainment is positively correlated with mothers who prioritize their children's education. An

empowerment and development cycle that benefits society at large is facilitated by this intergenerational effect.

12. Global development: Achieving the Sustainable Development Goals (SDGs) of the United Nations requires empowering women via education. It is widely acknowledged that tackling issues like gender inequality, hunger, poverty, and poor health requires a strong education system. Global inclusive growth and sustainable development are facilitated by our investments in women's education.

In conclusion, there is a close relationship between education and women's empowerment, with education acting as a spur for women to take on more leadership roles in their lives. Women can overcome obstacles, confront injustices, and actively participate in constructive social, economic, and political change when they receive the knowledge, skills, and opportunities that come with education. Encouragement of women's education is a step toward sustainable development and a better future for all, as well as an issue of equity and justice.

10. Conclusion: The Value of Honoring and Providing for Women;

The advancement and welfare of society heavily depend on women's respect and provision, which is why it is so valuable. The empowerment and support of women is essential for social, economic, and cultural development because they comprise almost half of the world's population.

Women should be treated with dignity and respect, as this is part of acknowledging their intrinsic worth. It entails valuing and honoring the accomplishments, contributions, and promise of women in a variety of industries, including the arts, business, science, politics, and education. By recognizing women's distinct viewpoints, skills, and abilities, we contribute to the creation of a society that is more equal and inclusive.

The provision of resources, opportunities, and rights for women to flourish is a key component of providing for them. This covers the following: political representation, legal protection, employment, fair wages, healthcare, and education. We address the structural obstacles and prejudices that impede women's advancement and keep them from realizing their full potential by providing for them.

Not to mention the fact that it is important to honor and support women:

1.Encouraging and supporting women contributes to gender equality, which is a basic human right. By ensuring that women have equal rights and opportunities to pursue their dreams, it aims to end discrimination and give them the freedom to follow their dreams.

2. Growth in the economy: Investing in and empowering women helps the economy as a whole. Women make important contributions to the workforce and their communities when they have an education, a job, and financial independence.

Research indicates that promoting gender parity in the workforce can boost innovation and productivity, ultimately resulting in financial progress.

3. Stability in society: Disparities in gender frequently make social tensions and injustices worse. Our society becomes more stable and cohesive when we address gender inequality and give women more opportunities. Stronger social ties, families, and communities are fostered when women are included and supported.

4. Better health and wellbeing: Women's health and well-being depend on having access to

high-quality healthcare and their right to procreate. Maternal health is improved, child mortality is decreased, and general health outcomes are enhanced when women's health needs are respected and met. Healthier families and communities are the result of our emphasis on women's health.

5. Diversity and representation: Respecting and assisting women guarantees their inclusion in leadership positions and decision-making processes. Strategies, policies, and governance are enhanced by the distinct perspectives and experiences that women bring to the table. All things considered, a more balanced and

diverse society produces better results.

6. Information and education: Enduring the poverty cycle and encouraging lifelong learning require respecting and facilitating women's educational opportunities. Women can gain the knowledge and abilities necessary to pursue careers, make educated decisions, and participate actively in society when they have access to high-quality education. Generational advancement is facilitated by educated women's favorable influence on their offspring's education.

7. Empowerment and self-worth: Women become more powerful and feel more valuable when they are respected and cared for. Women develop agency, confidence, and self-belief when they are treated with dignity, given equal opportunities, and support. Women who are empowered become agents of positive change, which has a knock-on effect on their families, communities, and next generation.

8. Enrichment of culture: Diversity and richness of culture are fostered by women's rights and honor. Traditions, values, and cultural heritage are vitally transmitted and preserved by women. By acknowledging their contributions

and offering venues for cultural expression, we make sure that different viewpoints are respected and valued, fostering a more vibrant and inclusive community.

9. Social justice: It is important to respect and care for women. Women have been disadvantaged and oppressed due to historical and systemic injustices, which must be addressed. We seek a just and fair society in which all people are treated with dignity, regardless of gender, and we actively work toward gender equity.

10. Sustainability: Achieving the goals of sustainable development requires respecting and assisting

women. In order to reduce poverty, create environmentally sustainable practices, and guarantee a resilient and prosperous future for all, women must be empowered, have equal access to resources, and participate in decision-making.

Recognizing that honoring and providing for women is a shared responsibility involving governments, organizations, communities, and individuals rather than just the women themselves is crucial. We make the world more fair, equitable, and prosperous for everyone when we value and give priority to the rights and well-being of women.